Galatians

At His Feet Studies

By Hope A. Blanton and Christine B. Gordon

19Baskets

Galatians
At His Feet Studies
© 2021 by Hope A. Blanton and Christine B. Gordon
ISBN 978-1-946862-15-0

19Baskets, Inc.
PO Box 31291
Omaha, NE 68131
https://19baskets.com

First Edition

Cover design by Sophie Calhoun

Photography by Jen Hinrichs

Endorsements

"Galatians is an ancient text for today's weary women. This study is an antidote to our age of self-help. God's Word, alongside Hope and Christine's commentary, bids us over and over to trust in Christ's finished work. What a relief; what good news. This is nourishment for the soul."

—**Jen Oshman**, author of *Enough About Me*

"The desire to add to the grace of Christ, to justify ourselves before God, sneaks into our lives more than we'd like to admit. Speaking to our dangerous temptation, Hope and Christine skillfully lead us through Galatians to remind us of the sufficiency of Christ's work and urge us to cling to faith in him. This study will support you with essential context, help you ask good questions, and call you to application. Reading their notes on Paul's letter, I found my heart delighting in the gospel and praying for transformation, exactly where I want a Bible study to lead me. May we delight in and be transformed by the truth of Galatians, led by this steady guide."

—**Taylor Turkington**, director of BibleEquipping, Bible teacher, DMin from Western Seminary

"Galatians is a book for the weary heart, and this study by At His Feet makes this book accessible for all students of the Bible. Whether you're seminary trained or opening your Bible for the first time, you'll find a home in the pages of Galatians! Hope and Christine walk through this book verse by verse in a rich and meaningful way, and help every reader see how God meets us in our failures and needs while pointing us to the hope of the gospel."

—**Amy Gannett**, M. Div, author, Bible teacher

"This is an excellent tool if you are longing to dig deep into the treasures of the Word of God! Hope and Christine will guide you into a practical, exciting, and enriching journey through the book of Galatians. Your affections will be stirred up for the gospel and your eyes fixed on Jesus. Ready for the ride? Jump in, you are in great company!"

—**Betsy Gómez**, author, blogger, supervisor for Media for Aviva Nuestros Corazones (Revive Our Hearts Hispanic Outreach)

Contents

At His Feet Story   1

User Guide   3

1. Deserting the Gospel of Grace: Galatians 1:1-10   5

2. Paul's Side of the Story: Galatians 1:11-2:10   17

3. Did Christ Die for Nothing? Galatians 2:11-21   27

4. The Unfair Trade: Galatians 3:1-14   37

5. From Slave to Son: Galatians 3:15-4:7   47

6. Why Are You Turning Back? Galatians 4:8-31   59

7. Freedom and the Spirit: Galatians 5   69

8. Boast in the Cross: Galatians 6   81

Acknowledgments   93

Notes   95

Works Cited   97

Other At His Feet Studies   99

At His Feet Story

A few years ago, Hope started looking for materials for the women's fall Bible study at our church. While she found a great number of quality Bible studies, she had a hard time finding studies written for women by women who were reformed. She also had a tough time finding in-depth studies of the Scripture that didn't take a whole lot of time. In a moment of desperation, Hope asked Chris if she would be willing to co-write a study on Romans, convincing her by asking, "I mean, really, how hard could it be?" And so it began. Weekly emails back and forth, Chris deep in commentaries, Hope mulling over questions, tweaking, editing, asking, pondering. A group of women at Redeemer Presbyterian Church in Lincoln, Nebraska, patiently bore with us as we experimented with them every week and learned to find our rhythm as writers.

Two years later, Hope approached Chris again, softening her up by telling her she could choose any book she wanted: 1 Samuel it was. Old Testament narrative is the best. Another study was born. About this time, women started asking us for copies of the two studies we had written. While we were trying to send endless pdfs to people around the country via email, a pastor friend who happens to be a publisher approached us at a party, offering to publish the Bible studies. Suddenly, we had a way to get these into the hands of women who could use them. This had been the point of the whole enterprise—to help make the Bible more accessible to women. But what would the name be?

During the first century, when Jesus walked the earth, a Jewish rabbi would have been surrounded by his students, with some of the men sitting as his feet to learn and listen. This was the custom, the understood norm of the day. But in Luke 10:39, *Mary* sat at the feet of Jesus. Mary, a woman, was taught by this unconventional rabbi. Mary was given the dignity of taking in his words, his pauses, his tone. To Jesus, she was every bit as worthy of his teaching as the men in the room were—and so are we, his women students today. And so we are At His Feet Bible Studies, hoping to sit at the feet of Jesus while we study his Word.

Please find our other available studies at our website:
www.athisfeetonline.com

User Guide

There is no right way to lead a Bible study. Every Bible study group is made up of different types of women with various sets of needs and dynamics. Below are some suggestions that might be helpful when using At His Feet Studies. Read it through. Use what you want. Forget the rest. We're glad you're here.

Participants Guide

This study is laid out like most commentaries. Each chapter is broken up into smaller portions with explanations of the verses in order. There are questions in the chapters before and after the commentary. The first set of questions are Observation Questions designed to help you interact with the basic content of the chapter. The second set of questions are Reflection Questions designed to help you engage your heart with the text in a vulnerable way.

Start by reading the Scripture passage noted at the top of the study page. Then answer the Observation Questions. Next, go back and read the Scripture side by side with the commentary, pausing between each grouping of verses to absorb both the commentary and the text more deeply. Then move on to answer the Reflection Questions.

Leaders Guide

There are eight questions for each study. When in a group setting, we suggest choosing your favorite Reflection Questions to focus on, especially if you run short on time. If you have more time feel free to work through all the questions. For those groups where people have not had the time and space to read through the commentary and questions, you can simply read the commentary out loud at the beginning of your time. That way all women can participate. We always suggest reading the Scripture passage out loud before you begin.

Extras

The focus verse is something to spend time reflecting on since it's the heart of the passage. Consider memorizing it individually or as a group.

Use the section we have labeled "Reflections, curiosities, frustrations" to write down things about the text that seem confusing to you or hard for you to wrap your brain around. This is meant to give you space to express how you're a work in progress as you work through this text and engage with God's Word.

Study 1

Deserting the Gospel of Grace

"I feel like I'm failing. I can't even seem to stop yelling at my kids or stay on track reading the Bible, let alone lead a ministry." Julia had been a believer for years, coming to know Christ in her twenties, and now was in a place of leadership. She took her faith seriously and had decided that if she was to be an example, her own life, including her spiritual practices, had to be consistently in order. She had known years of joy with the Lord. She was filled with gratitude when she first became a Christian, overwhelmed by the free gift of grace. She received Christ's righteousness with a grateful heart and knew she had nothing to add or contribute to her salvation. But that season seemed further and further away as she took on responsibilities and pushed herself to grow. Her joy, freedom, and grateful heart slowly turned to anxiety, comparison, and shame. What had gone wrong?

Julia's story is a common one; without understanding why, Christians sometimes begin to experience burnout and a coldness in their faith. Many start by faith, receiving the gift of grace, but as the years go by and life gets more complicated, they begin to attempt to justify themselves to God by something other than faith in the one who saved them. They strive to add badges of honor to their resume of spiritual achievements, growing a list of accomplishments in order to make themselves worthy in the eyes of God and others. Added to their faith in Jesus are things like wearing the right clothing, being with the right people, or choosing the right type of schooling for their children. But there is pressure to do more, to up their status in their faith. And so they might host the monthly women's gathering or volunteer for the

5

food pantry. They may also begin to see those who do not have such practices as "entry-level Christians," not as serious about their faith. If they fail in their disciplines, they feel unable to approach God, unworthy of his attention. Their relationship to him becomes less about what he has freely given them and more about what they do for him. They may feel harried, burdened, and pressured to keep pace with whomever happens to be setting the standard of the "faithful Christian" in their crowd.

Faith in Jesus + something else = how we get into and stay in God's kingdom. This is a formula that is not only discouraging but, as Paul will tell us in Galatians, completely opposes the gospel. We are saved by faith alone as we respond to God's free gift of grace. This never changes, no matter how long we are believers. And yes, we must respond to this gift by working out our salvation (Philippians 2:12), but any work we do is the result of the Holy Spirit working in us, strengthening us, making us able to obey (Philippians 2:13). We are not saved and then get left by God to work out our Christian life on our own. We do not get into the kingdom and then try to "level up" by our works. All of our growth is of grace. By listening in to Paul's conversation with the Galatian church, we will find freedom and our own way back to the gospel as the only motivator and fuel for our growth in Christ.

Historical Context

Read Acts 13–14

Before it was a book in our Bible, Galatians was a letter, written by Paul to a group of churches in a region known as Galatia. Galatians, Paul's first existing letter, is one of the most occasional letters in the New Testament, meaning that it was written for a very specific set of circumstances taking place in the churches of the region. To understand Paul's passion and why he is writing, we must first understand how the churches came to be.

Paul had taken his first missionary journey through the southern part of present-day Turkey, between the Black Sea and the Mediterranean Sea. He had established churches in the region, specifically in the cities of Psidian Antioch, Iconium, Lystra, and Derbe. Acts 13 and 14 chronicle the travels of Paul and Barnabas throughout the region of Galatia. In the city called Psidian Antioch (different from the Antioch where Paul's home church was located), the Gentiles rejoiced and believed, but the Jews were jealous and eventually ran Paul and his people out of town (Acts 13:13-52). At Iconium, "a great number of both Jews and Greeks believed" (Acts 14:1), and a church was established during a long visit. However, some people of the city disagreed with the apostles and were determined to stone them, causing Paul and Barnabas to flee to Lystra and Derbe. When Paul healed a man in Lystra, the people there decided he and Barnabas were Greek gods and tried to worship them. Paul corrected them and established a church there as well.

Jews from other cities where Paul had preached were angered by his teaching and came to Lystra to stop him. They stoned him, drug him out of the city, and left him for dead. But Paul, preserved by God, got up and went to yet another city, Derbe, where he and Barnabas founded another church. On their way back to their home church of Antioch, they went back through all of the newly established churches, encouraging them with fasting and prayer and appointing elders for each. All of this happened sometime between 45 and 48 AD, about twelve years after Christ ascended into heaven. Most experts date the letter of Galatians around the same time, meaning Paul was writing this emotionally charged letter just one or two years after having started the churches. Why? Paul begins the proper part of his letter with the words "I am astonished" and sprinkle in phrases like "O foolish

Galatians!" and "You were running well. Who hindered you from obeying the truth?" What has him so upset?

Apparently Paul was not the only teacher influencing the churches of Galatia. After he and Barnabas left, a group of teachers known as the Judaizers came to the region and began teaching what they would have thought of as the "next level" of the faith. It was fine that the Gentiles, or non-Jews, of the area had become Christians; these new converts had gotten a good start in the faith. But in order to progress, said these false teachers, they would need to add something to their newfound faith—the ceremonial Jewish law. Gentile converts were being required not only to be circumcised, a Jewish requirement under the covenant of Moses, but also to follow the entire law of Moses. God's moral law, summarized in the Ten Commandments, is timeless, perpetual, and enduring. By God's moral law, he teaches sinners that we have fallen short of God's glory, and that the only way to be forgiven of our sins and reconciled to him is through faith alone. Then, by that same moral law, God teaches his redeemed and reconciled people in all ages how to live lives that please him.

On the other hand, the ceremonial laws (related to worship) and civil laws (related to the kingdom) only served a temporary purpose of pointing forward to the coming Messiah. Once Christ came, he fulfilled all those laws in his birth, life, death, and resurrection, abolishing them from further use. The problem was that these religious teachers were acknowledging that getting into the kingdom by faith alone was acceptable but that to stay in the kingdom, much less to "progress," the Gentile believers needed to supplement their faith with some specific actions—specifically, with the ceremonial laws that Jesus had already fulfilled. Continuing in the faith meant Jesus plus something else.

Paul's response in the letter of Galatians has left us his most heated letter. He is "astonished," "perplexed," and in the "pains of childbirth" for their faith once again. He explains that this is not just some marginal issue but a central matter of life and death, heaven and hell. This letter, though written to a specific group of people at a specific time for a specific reason, has been part of the foundation of our faith for hundreds of years. Martin Luther loved it so much he called it his "wife." Tim Keller writes, "The book of Galatians is dynamite." As we study Paul's words to the churches he planted, we will be reminded that it's Jesus plus nothing and rejoice.

Read Galatians 1:1-10

Observation Questions

1. In verses 6-7 what does Paul say he is astonished by?

2. In verses 8-9 what does Paul say should happen to anyone preaching a false gospel, no matter who it is?

3. What questions does Paul ask in verse 10? How does he answer them for himself?

Verses 1-5. Right out of the gate, Paul makes the source of his authority clear. Jesus Christ himself, not men, appointed him to the task of making disciples. Therefore he did not need the approval or endorsement of the other apostles in Jerusalem. Normally in his letters, Paul says something positive about the recipients in his "To" line. Here, he makes no encouraging remarks about the churches in Galatia. If we continue reading, we will find that he doesn't have anything positive to say. Instead, he moves directly into praise to God, where he emphasizes the fact that Jesus "delivered us" (ESV) or "rescued us" (NIV). The Galatians, along with all of us, were desperate, helpless, and weak when Christ came to our rescue. God's initiative is the only thing that saves us.

Verses 6-10. Now Paul comes to the reason for his letter. He cannot believe that these dear brothers and sisters, whom he so recently saw enter the kingdom through faith, are turning away from Jesus. It may seem at a casual glance that this is a small theological quarrel. Paul makes it clear that this is so much more. To pervert the gospel, says Paul, is to walk away from Jesus completely. Verse 6 mentions that the Galatians were called "in the grace of Christ," not in the obedience of the law or in their best efforts. Adding anything to grace is a distortion. Paul goes so far as to tell them that it doesn't matter who preaches something different or what kind of authority they seem to have: If anyone preaches a different gospel, what they teach will lead people to hell. Paul repeats himself for emphasis: Entrance into the kingdom and life in the kingdom is through faith and faith alone. Anything different than that will send you to hell. Obviously, Paul is trying to please God and not men, as he argues in verse 10. He sees himself as a slave, as someone who belongs to another. Therefore, he seeks to please Christ, his master.

As we continue to listen in to the conversation between Paul and these baby churches, a couple of things have already become clear. Both we and the Galatians need deliverance and a rescuer. That deliverance came in the form of a person who chose to save us at great cost to himself. Requiring anything in addition to faith in Jesus's work is not, in fact, the gospel but something else entirely. And so we will begin to examine our hearts as we listen to Paul to see if we are trusting Christ's work alone for our salvation and growth.

A note to the reader: Paul, here and in other letters, refers to the first-century practice of slavery, which was widespread in his day and often involved people selling themselves into service in order to repay a debt. He uses slavery as a metaphor to describe a person's relationship to what or whom they worship—either God or the law.

At no time is it appropriate to use any references to slavery in the Bible to justify cruel treatment or ownership of another human made in God's image. Nor is it appropriate to twist the Bible's meaning in order to condone the wicked system of chattel slavery as it was practiced in the United States.

Please feel free to look back to this note as you make your way through Galatians and encounter Paul's many references to slavery.

Reflection Questions

4. What part of the background and history behind Galatians stood out to you?

How fast the false teachers moved in.

5. What do you make of all the resistance to the gospel Paul experienced?

The perseverance and forward progress of the church will always be hard work.

6. Paul had poured into starting and caring for the Galatian church, even to the point of great physical harm to himself, only to find them turning away from the true gospel. What emotion do you think he felt as a result? How would you feel if you were him?

It is just JESUS. The work is already complete.

⤷ RELIEF, HOPE

7. Paul makes the shocking claim that to pervert the gospel by adding anything to grace alone is the same as walking away from Jesus completely. What about this makes you feel uncomfortable or nervous? What about it makes you feel relieved?

8. The Galatians and many of us live with the equation faith in Jesus + something else = how we get into and stay in God's kingdom, even though this is not the truth of the gospel. What is the "something else" that you personally add? When and why did that start?

What is my "something else"
↳ being needed
↳ my kids being great, believers

Focus verse: *I am astonished that you are so quickly deserting him who called you in the grace of Christ and are turning to a different gospel— not that there is another one, but there are some who trouble you and want to distort the gospel of Christ.*
Galatians 1:6–7

Reflections, curiosities, frustrations:

Study 2

Paul's Side of the Story

Read Galatians 1:11-2:10

Observation Questions

1. Write down all the details we learn in chapter 1, verses 11-17, about Paul before and after his conversion.

2. How many years after his conversion did Paul go to Jerusalem? What would people say about him when he would visit churches in Judea? (See chapter 1, verses 18-24.)

3. List all the people who are named and what you learn about each of them in chapter 2, verses 1-10.

This next section of Galatians reads like an autobiography of Paul, filling in some gaps in the timeline of his life. It can sound defensive or even arrogant, leaving us to wonder why Paul would seek to prove himself and his credentials to this young church. Was Paul feeling insecure? Was he competing with the apostles in Jerusalem for popularity or a following? If we dig a bit into his historical context, we will see that Paul was actually defending the gospel. He was doing so by defending his own apostleship, which he begins to explain in chapter 1, verse 11. The backstory for this passage is that some false teachers came to Galatia after Paul founded the church and began teaching that the gospel was a good start but that to advance in the faith, believers must add something to it. Specifically, they must live like Jews by observing certain ceremonial food laws and being circumcised. Paul wanted to argue against this and bring them back to the true faith—the gospel alone, through faith in Jesus alone. The false brothers (see Galatians 2:4) may have been discounting Paul's apostleship and preaching. Scholars believe these men were telling those in the Galatian church that Paul initially received the gospel from the apostles in Jerusalem but that when he began to teach others, he mistakenly left off a few requirements, including circumcision. The false brothers wanted to offer correction to that gospel, offering the "whole package," including following the ceremonial Mosaic Law.

But Paul did not receive the gospel from the apostles in Jerusalem. In fact, he didn't receive the gospel from any man; he met Jesus himself on the road to Damascus. Paul takes the rest of chapter 1 and the first part of chapter 2 to convince the Galatians of the divine origin of his apostleship and his subsequent ministry. He then goes on to explain his relationship to the leaders of the church in Jerusalem and their partnership with him.

Chapter 1, verses 11–17. The gospel was not new information to Paul. He would have been familiar with what was taught about Jesus when he was trying to destroy the church before his conversion. Paul was living the life of a successful, devoted Jew, convinced that he was pleasing God by attempting to annihilate the followers of Jesus. He was so uncompromising in his determination to keep the law that he advanced past some of his peers. Paul makes it clear that he did not come to faith because of someone's clever argument or further explanation of the gospel. Paul had a supernatural encounter with the Son of God. Paul was purposefully and doggedly working with all of his power to wipe out Jesus's church when Jesus himself met him on the road.

Verse 16 tells us that God was "pleased" to reveal his Son to Paul. Paul was not a threat to God and his kingdom. He was not someone who had to be dealt with before he did too much damage to the church. No, God set Paul apart before he was born (verse 15) and revealed Jesus to him so that he might "preach him among the Gentiles." Paul's training, including his extensive knowledge and experience with the Scriptures, was part of what God used to build his church. This is often what God has done in history through his saints. Think of Joseph living in a prison in Egypt, then being used to save so many during the famine. God can use anyone anytime, including a zealous Jew who was determined to destroy all Christians. Paul's meeting with the Lord was both a conversion and a commissioning to preach. And though he was suddenly on the

19

same "team" as the Jerusalem apostles, he did not visit them at that time. Instead he went to Arabia, where most commentators assume he began preaching the gospel.

Chapter 1, verses 18-24. Paul goes on with his history of apostleship. He did eventually go to Jerusalem for a short visit with Peter (also known as Cephas) and James but was generally not known by the churches in that area. In fact, the Jerusalem church was speaking of Paul as a sort of legend. Paul was not a student of the Jerusalem church's theology. He was a former enemy who was now preaching the faith. They were not correcting him but glorifying God because of him. Paul is proving the point here again that he didn't receive his information from the Jerusalem church; he received it directly from Christ.

Chapter 2, verses 1-9. Paul continues his narrative explaining that he had a revelation from God and went to Jerusalem in response. He was not summoned by the leaders of the church there; nor did he need to be corrected by them. In fact, he went to be sure that he "was not running or had not run in vain." What does he mean by this? Paul was worried not that he had the wrong message but that there might be a split between the Jews and the Gentiles in the church. This time when he went to Jerusalem, he took Titus, a Gentile who was uncircumcised. He wanted the brothers to see in the flesh that it was the gospel alone that saved, not any adherence to Mosaic Law.

Why was circumcision such a big deal? Circumcision in the Old Testament was part of what was known as the ceremonial law, a group of laws concerning how one dressed, what one ate, and other practices that made a person either "clean" or "unclean" and therefore able or unable to go to the temple and worship God. Gentiles were generally considered unclean as a people, since they did not adhere to these strict codes that were followed by Jews.

These laws were originally put in place to set apart the nation of Israel and to show the holiness of God. Ultimately, these laws also foreshadowed Christ's coming in various ways. God gave the ceremonial laws to demonstrate the impossibility of making oneself acceptable before such a holy God, and to point the people to faith in the coming Messiah alone for their salvation. Unfortunately, the false brothers were using these laws opposite of how God had intended them—to avoid putting their faith fully in Christ by thinking they could justify themselves through their religious performances.

Though it wouldn't seem like a big deal to us, it would have been shocking to Jewish Christians that a non-Jew such as Titus was now considered clean, able to stand in the presence of God and worship, simply because of the work of Christ. The false brothers probably expected and desired Peter and James to reject Titus, and therefore Paul. But Paul is telling us that if he compromised at this point, if he said, "Yes, you may proceed. Circumcise Titus; that will make him a true believer," he would have missed the gospel altogether and been once again enslaved to the whole law. If Paul added something to the gospel, he would have ended up right back where he started: trying to zealously keep the law in order to make God love him. Anytime we try to find some avenue to God other than his free grace alone, it only leads to slavery. Paul had been willing to circumcise Timothy in order to gain access to share the gospel of Jesus with unbelieving Jews, who would not associate with anyone uncircumcised (Acts 16:3). Here, though, these were professing Christians insisting upon circumcision. If Paul went along with it, circumcision would enslave Gentile believers to the ceremonial law and distort the gospel.

Instead of rejecting him, James, Peter, and other influential apostles in Jerusalem saw that Paul had been called to preach to the non-Jews, just as they had been called to preach to the Jews. They accepted Paul's ministry, not changing any of his teaching. It was important that the Galatians understood this validation and acceptance of Paul's ministry by the Jerusalem church. There was one gospel, not two. However, there were separate spheres of work and influence, given to these men by God. The gospel ministry would look different among Jews than it would look among Gentiles.

Chapter 2, verse 10. Why suddenly this mention of the poor? Poverty in the ancient world was extreme, with no social welfare and no national healthcare system. Those who begged along the road were sometimes given alms by the wealthy, but the suffering for anyone crippled or otherwise unable to work was miserable. From the beginning of the church, Christians supplied food and other needs for the poor, choosing deacons in Acts 6:1-7 to be sure that everyone received what they needed. Both Paul and the Jerusalem apostles were convinced that this help must continue as part of the church's work.

A couple of things stand out as warnings in this passage. First, we can be incredibly zealous, hard-working, and committed to God and at the same time be working against him if we are not in Christ. Second, good intentions, morality, and law-keeping do not save. Only Jesus's work makes us clean and able to be in God's presence. Third, though ministry must always carry the same message, it may use different methods, depending on its recipients. Finally, there will always be some group of people trying to convince us that true Christianity involves Jesus plus x, y, and z. We must never trust in anything to gain us favor with God other than Jesus's work on our behalf, not when we first meet him and not when we've known him for many years.

Reflection Questions

4. Which parts of Paul's personal story surprised you? Which parts are you curious about and wish you had more information?

5. What does it tell us about God's character that he would take an exceptionally devout Jew who was persecuting Christians and transform him into someone who would take that same gospel to the Gentiles? Do you know anyone who has had a radical conversion story?

6. Before Paul was converted, he was persecuting Christians. The Judaizers were preaching a false gospel. Both thought they were working zealously for God but were far from him. Who have you seen operate like this? Why did they?

7. Because Titus was a Gentile convert who wasn't doing "Jesus + circumcision = how we get into and stay in God's kingdom" as they wanted him to, they counted him as unclean, even though he was a believer. When have you judged a brother or sister this way, deeming them "unclean" even though they were trusting Jesus for salvation? Is there anything you need to repent of?

8. When James, Peter, and Paul met, they accepted each other and realized that they had the same goal of preaching the gospel, but to different people groups and by different means. When have you seen ministries that are very different accomplish the same goal of sharing the gospel? Did you consider one more godly than the other?

Focus verse: *And I was still unknown in person to the churches of Judea that are in Christ. They only were hearing it said, "He who used to persecute us is now preaching the faith he once tried to destroy." And they glorified God because of me.*
Galatians 1:22-24

Reflections, curiosities, frustrations:

Study 3

Did Christ Die for Nothing?

Read Galatians 2:11-21

Observation Questions

1. In verses 11–14 why was Paul upset with Cephas (Peter)?

2. Summarize what verses 15–16 are saying about the law.

3. Rewrite verses 17–21 in your own words.

Verses 11–14. It seemed everything was going well: Peter and the Jerusalem apostles had their mission to the Jews. Paul and Barnabas had their mission to the Gentiles. Everyone agreed to take care of the poor. So why does verse 11 begin with Paul confronting Cephas (Peter) so publicly and forcefully? Remember that the center of Christianity at the time was Jerusalem. Paul's home church was at Antioch, a city between three and four hundred miles northeast of Jerusalem, depending on your walking path. (Antioch, now Antakya, is in modern-day Turkey.) Apparently Peter had come to Antioch for an extended visit and had gotten quite used to eating meals and probably taking communion with the Gentile Christians. This was not the norm for Jews, as they would have always separated themselves from any "unclean" Gentiles, fearing that they might be "contaminated" by them and therefore unable to approach God or his temple. But Peter had had a vision in Acts 10 where God showed him that all foods were now clean, even the pork, shellfish, and certain birds that Jews avoided because of Old Testament ceremonial food laws. He had begun exercising this new freedom among the brothers in Antioch. This was such a radical change that the people who practiced it needed a new name. Acts 11:26 records these words describing Paul and Barnabas: "For a whole year they met with the church and taught a great many people. And in Antioch the disciples were first called

28

Christians." God had made a new people out of what used to be two very divided groups. This was his church, his people, the new Israel. And Peter was living out his faith in a practical way by eating with his new Christian brothers, non-Jews who did not follow the dietary laws of his Jewish heritage.

But Peter's gospel practice did not last. When "certain men came from James" (verse 12), Peter stopped eating with the Gentiles out of fear of backlash from the Jews who had been converted to Christ but still strictly adhered to Jewish cultural norms about meals and circumcision. What was worse, the "rest of the Jews" (verse 13) followed Peter's lead and separated themselves from the Gentiles as well. Even Barnabas, who had been Paul's partner, was led astray. Why did Paul call this hypocrisy? It's because Peter did not forget what was true about his freedom in Christ; nor did he suddenly question whether he could eat with Gentiles and be clean in God's eyes. Instead, what Peter questioned was whether he could eat with Gentile brothers and still have the same good standing in the eyes of the Jews. Peter was afraid his position in the church might be compromised. He was under immense pressure from the mother church in Jerusalem and so he acted not in faith, not in line with the gospel, but in fear of what others might think.

Paul saw what was happening and called Peter out, naming his hypocrisy. The laws that had once been the way God set apart the nation of Israel for his use and to point toward his holiness had been totally fulfilled in Jesus. It was no longer what they ate or with whom they ate that determined their ability to approach God, and Peter knew this. When Peter suddenly stopped eating with the Gentiles, he was effectively acting again like a Jew in order to avoid problems with other Jews. Peter was acting like a coward, and Paul called him on it.

Imagine how these Gentile brothers must have felt. They correctly understood that they were acceptable to God simply because of their faith in Christ. But Peter's actions spoke volumes: "You may be good enough for Jesus and good enough to be saved, but you're not good enough for us; to be truly clean and accepted, not only must you believe in Christ but you also must become culturally and ceremonially Jewish."

We may shake our heads at what seem to be insignificant practices to us, held onto by people who clearly did not understand the heart of the gospel. But don't we do the same? Don't we hold up parts of our culture, even our church culture, as requirements for entry into fellowship or even the household of faith? You may be saved by faith alone, but if you're a real Christian, you'll study the Bible a certain way, educate your children a certain way, or vote a certain way, and so on. The list is endless. We must be careful that we do not require more than Jesus does and that our practices do not create division in the church.

Verses 15–19. Paul was in the middle of speaking to Peter in verse 14, and since the original Greek language did not use quotation marks, there is debate about where the quote stops. Whether he is still quoting himself directly or only recounting his words to Peter for the sake of the Galatians, Paul continues his explanation of why Peter was wrong to stop eating with the Gentiles. The "we" in verse 15 refers to Peter and Paul. Jews did have some privilege, and they knew it. They were recipients of the covenant and the Torah. They had a path to being made clean before God, which is what the food laws were really about. Gentiles were understood to be "sinners" with no way to cleanliness other than converting to become Jews. Yet, says Paul in verse 16, even we, the Jews, know that we cannot be justified by anything but faith in Christ.

This is the first time he uses the word "justified," a very significant word not only in the book of Galatians but in the entire Bible. What does it mean? To be justified is to be counted righteous before God, to receive an acquittal from sin and also to be given the record of Jesus. This could not happen through keeping the law, although if anyone had ever tried, it was Paul. Justification could then and can now only happen through faith in Christ.

In verse 17 we begin to sense that Paul is arguing with someone, though we're not sure whom. This is where a technique called mirror reading becomes helpful. Mirror reading is the process of trying to infer what we don't have—the background or the other side of the letter—from what we do have. It seems that Paul's actions of eating with "Gentile sinners" who didn't follow Jewish food laws was bothering the Jews in Jerusalem. They must have begun asking, "Well, if Christ does not require the keeping of the law, does he encourage us to sin all we want?" "May it never be!" says Paul, in very strong language. If he rebuilds the practices of ceremonial law-keeping he used to rely on before he knew Christ to please God, he'll just prove how he cannot keep the law. In fact, Paul says in verse 19 that he "died to the law." In other words, Paul stopped using the law as a way to be saved.

Verses 20–21. Obviously Paul had not been physically killed like Jesus on the cross. But he had died to an entire way of life and was now united to Christ. And this unity, this "in Christ-ness," meant something very serious to Paul, as it should to us. If we are united to him, everything that is his has become ours, including his obedience during life on this earth, his crucifixion, his resurrection, and his ascension. He has given us his status, his standing, his record. In the sentence translated "I have been crucified," Paul uses a verb in the perfect tense, which signifies a state that was true and continues to be true. The voice is passive, meaning it was done to him. And the mood is indicative, meaning this is not a command but a statement of truth about him. Paul did not earn this status, but he was given this status through faith in Christ. Practically, this means that God treats Paul, and us, as if we died on the cross and paid for every sin. We get his track record, his account, his earnings, his past. "Now when I live," explains Paul, "I live by faith, knowing how much I am loved." To "nullify" is to invalidate or abolish. Trying to earn righteousness or rightness with God through obeying the law would be to invalidate God's grace, making his death purposeless. As Tim Keller writes, "If anyone could be saved by being good, Christ's death was for nothing."

Did you get that? When God looks for your worthiness, he sees Jesus's achievements. It's as if he checks on your bank account balance of goodness and Jesus's is displayed instead. He looks at your history of kindness, holiness, and justice and sees Jesus's in place of yours. This is good news, and trying to replace the perfect Son of Man's track record with your own efforts is just silly. We can now live, as Paul writes, "by faith in the Son of God, who loved me and gave himself up for me."

Reflection Questions

4. The Jews had to follow the law, then Christ freed them from it, then they still returned to it. What do you think was going on in their hearts for this to happen? When does this happen in your heart?

5. In this passage we see Peter (Cephas) acting like a coward when certain believers come around, fearing them more than the truth of the gospel. When do you struggle with this type of fear of man?

6. Peter's choice to follow the law again communicated to Gentile Christians that they were inferior to Jewish Christians, which was a lie. When have you followed a certain seemingly Christian practice that made others feel that they didn't measure up?

7. When Christ was crucified it was like we were crucified with him. Why does this matter?

8. When God looks at your "spiritual bank account" he sees Jesus. In what areas of your life do you connect with this truth? In what areas do you struggle to believe that?

Focus verse: *I have been crucified with Christ. It is no longer I who live, but Christ who lives in me. And the life I now live in the flesh I live by faith in the Son of God, who loved me and gave himself for me. I do not nullify the grace of God, for if righteousness were through the law, then Christ died for no purpose.*
Galatians 2:20–21

Reflections, curiosities, frustrations:

Study 4

The Unfair Trade

Read Galatians 3:1-14

Observation Questions

1. In verses 1-6 Paul asks six questions. What is he asking about? What point is he trying to make?

2. Read Genesis 12:1-3. How does it add to what you read in verses 7-9?

3. Define the word *cursed*. Who does Paul say in verse 10 is under a curse? And who became the curse (verse 13)?

Verses 1-6. "O foolish Galatians!" Why the harsh words? Paul seems baffled at the Galatians' current misunderstanding of the gospel as he reminds them of their past. First, he recollects that through clear and vivid preaching, he explained to them the crucifixion, so that Jesus was "publicly portrayed" as crucified. Then, they received the Holy Spirit, not by "works of the law," human actions done to obey Old Testament law, but by "hearing with faith."

So what did the Galatians do initially to receive the gift of the Holy Spirit? They heard the gospel and believed. That was it; that was their contribution in joining the kingdom of God. They listened and trusted. They heard the truth of the crucifixion and put their trust in the one who was crucified.

"Has someone cast a spell on you?" asks Paul in verse 3. It's as if he's asking them, "If you were born by means of the Spirit into the life of faith, why are you switching over to some other method for growth in your faith?" Paul is telling these saints that the way they grow in the kingdom must be the same way they entered the kingdom—by faith in Christ, and through the power of the Spirit. To try to please God by carefully performing works of the ceremonial law in the strength of their own flesh, instead of trusting Christ by power of the Spirit would be "in vain," as he writes in verse 4.

The word translated "supplies" in the ESV and "give" in the NIV expresses the idea of a generous amount. God gives a generous portion of the Spirit to believers, as evidenced by the miracles the Galatians apparently had seen in their own church. Paul's rhetorical question in verse 5 forces them to remember that God supplied the Spirit to them "by hearing with faith." Then Paul continues to make his case for faith by referencing Abraham. Abraham was the patriarch, the father of Judaism, revered by the Jews as the ultimate example of obedience. Paul points here not to his law-keeping but to his faith. In Genesis 15, God told Abraham that his offspring would be as many as the stars, though at the time he had no children. Abraham believed God, and God counted it to Abraham's account as righteousness. God treated Abraham as if he were righteous at that moment, even though he was still unrighteous both in his heart and in his behavior. Faith, not works, made Abraham right with God.

Verses 7–9. In verse 7, it appears that Paul is again answering his opponents whose words we do not get to read. Apparently they were telling new Galatian believers that the way to be a son of Abraham was to follow the law. Paul tells them instead that they had already become sons of Abraham by faith. He goes on to quote Genesis 12, explaining that God showed Abraham that he was going to bless not just the Jews but all ethnicities and cultures through him and his children. Abraham trusted God's words. So then, those Galatians who trusted God were blessed like Abraham. We, then, are children of Abraham, not because of our bloodline, but because we trust God. We may be Puerto Rican, Lebanese, or Canadian. None of these give us any advantage or disadvantage in terms of growing in our faith or in being heirs to this wonderful promise given to Abraham. The way we are saved is the same way Abraham was saved and the same way the Gentiles were saved—by faith in God's promise to save us.

Verses 10–14. Paul finishes this section by talking about blessings and curses, using multiple texts from the law itself. First he explains that trying to rest in your good works will ultimately put you under a curse. Why? You can't do enough good works, and you cannot do them perfectly, which is the requirement for any access or connection to God. He quotes Deuteronomy 27:26, emphasizing that "all things" in the Book of the Law must be done. There is no grading on a curve if you're trying to get to God by good works. You either do all of the things, and do them perfectly, or you fail. In verse 11 Paul quotes Habbakuk 2:4, explaining that faith, not the law, is the way to be justified before God. Verse 12 includes a quote from Leviticus 18:5. The law isn't received like a free gift; the law involves work. The law is not something you trust in; it's something you do.

The law has cursed us because we cannot obey it fully. Without Jesus, we are doomed to be judged by God according to our obedience, which is flawed. But Christ "redeemed us from the curse." This word, *redemption*, has a rich meaning. It comes from the world of warfare. In ancient times, once a battle had been won, some men would inevitably be taken from the losing side as slaves by the winners. Those with importance and wealth would be held with a ransom as their countrymen came up with the money to buy back their freedom. The process of buying the men back was called redemption. This is what Christ did with his life; he bought us back from being slaves to sin. Paul quotes Deuteronomy 21:23 to explain how Jesus became a curse for us. Jews did not consider that someone was cursed because they had been hung on a tree; rather, Jews hung people on a tree to show that they had already been cursed. Surely Paul is referring to this as he writes about Jesus hanging on a tree. Jesus became a curse for us; he took the curse of the law for us.

And what do we get in return for him taking our curse? His blessing. That blessing that was promised to the Gentiles through

Abraham comes to us. That's the exchange. Jesus took our curse, and we get his blessing—the Spirit that comes through faith. But it's not just that he took our sin and we therefore came back to zero, to neutral. He also then gave us his righteousness, his blessing, so that now we are treated by God as if we had acted in every situation with Christ's integrity, Christ's righteousness, Christ's right motives.

So what does this mean for us in a practical sense? How do we appropriate this standing before God as we seek to grow as Christians? It means that if we have trusted in Christ for salvation, we start each day knowing we are already accepted. We walk through the day knowing that when we yell at our children, disrespect our bosses, or covet in our hearts, our "account of righteousness" does not decrease. Our standing before God does not change. Even in the moments we are yelling, disrespecting, or coveting, God still sees our record as if we acted faithfully, with utmost righteousness. As if we spoke with perfect love to our children and boss. As if we looked at all the good and beautiful things without a trace of coveting in our hearts.

How is this possible? Aren't we still sinners in that moment? Yes. Sinners who walk around with Christ's record before God. Sound unfair? It absolutely is. But the gospel isn't fair; the gospel is a gift—a ridiculous exchange of Jesus's obedience for our sin. Do not, Paul would tell us even now, do not go back to some other way of trying to achieve a good reputation with God. The only way to achieve a good status with God is by faith in Christ's status. For the Galatians, life now had to be ordered not by careful keeping of Jewish ceremonies but upon the immovable foundation of Christ's righteousness. This is called passive righteousness, and it is the only place we can find total security from which to live by faith. Because we are already enough in Christ, we do not need to find our status or worth in our perfectly dressed and sculpted body, our mindfulness practice, our tastefully decorated and clean home, or our well-behaved children. We as individuals and as a church may live as completely loved and cherished people, just as Paul is exhorting the Galatians to do.

Reflection Questions

4. Faith applied through the Spirit saves, not doing works of the law. Why is it easier to trust our "doing" versus our "believing"?

5. In this passage Paul magnifies the truth that trying to be accepted by God through good works will actually bring a curse. What about that is different than what you were taught? Who taught you that?

6. *Redemption* is an ancient wartime term that meant buying back your people who've been captured by the enemy. In what ways does the context behind this word change your view of Christ's redemption of you?

7. When Christ gave you his righteousness he didn't just take your sin away but gave you blessing in its place. How does that alter or add to your understanding of the gospel?

8. The gospel is an unfair exchange that makes us always accepted before God every day, no exceptions. Do you believe this? Why or why not?

Focus verse: *Let me ask you only this: Did you receive the Spirit by works of the law or by hearing with faith? Are you so foolish? Having begun by the Spirit, are you now being perfected by the flesh?*
Galatians 3:2–3

Reflections, curiosities, frustrations:

Study 5

From Slave to Son

Read Galatians 3:15-4:7

Observation Questions

1. Summarize what chapter 3, verses 15–18, are saying about promise versus law.

2. According to chapter 3, verse 19, why was the law given? Who put it in place?

3. What do chapter 3, verses 21-29, say about the law? About faith?

4. From chapter 4, verses 1-7, describe what Christ did and what impact that had on the recipients.

Chapter 3, verses 15-22. Remember that in the first part of chapter 3, Paul forcefully reminded the Galatians that they were saved and that they received the Spirit through faith, not by following the law. He then explained to them that trying to follow the law to earn salvation brings a curse, while all of us can receive the blessing promised to Abraham if we are like him in the way that he trusted in God's promises. Now Paul argues from a different angle—that of a covenant. The Jews understood from Genesis 15 that God had made a covenant with Abraham, promising that Abraham's descendants would be as many as the stars and that they would possess the land (Genesis 15:17-21). Abraham believed God. Take a minute and read Genesis 17:1-8, where God reminded Abraham of this covenant and gave him just a little more insight into it.

Beginning in verse 16, Paul refers to this Genesis 17 passage and, little by little, talks the Galatians through it. The promises, he argues, were made to Abraham and a single seed, an outstanding person in a long line of people born to the descendants of Abraham. This particular, special "offspring" is Christ, says Paul. The ultimate blessing that came from God's promise to Abraham was the Savior of the world, Jesus. This was how God would bless all of the nations of the world through Abraham, by making one of his great-great-great-grandchildren Jesus himself.

So what are verses 15, 17, and 18 talking about? Another way to read verse 15 might be, "Let's use an example from everyday life: even with a will, no one cancels it or adds things to it once everyone has signed it." To set a helpful paradigm, think about this scenario. Let's say your grandfather owns an apple orchard. One day he says to you, "When I die, you will inherit the apple orchard." What must you do to get that orchard? All you really need to do is trust the word of your grandfather enough to show up and take possession of the orchard when he dies. The land is a gift to you, with no requirements or prerequisites for your possession. Now, imagine that while your grandfather is still living, he gives you a handbook for caring for the orchard. Now how do you come to possess the vineyard? The same way you would have before you got the handbook and regardless of whether or not you followed it. The vineyard is a gift to you, an inheritance when your grandfather dies. You cannot earn that orchard by using the handbook any more than you did the day he wrote your name in his will. You get the orchard either way because he promised it to you.

This is what Paul is saying in verses 17 and 18. God made Abraham a promise, and he ratified it in Genesis 15 by appearing as a flaming torch moving through the halves of animals. Effectively, he was saying to Abraham, "May it be done to me as it was to the animals if I do not keep this promise to you and your descendants." For 430 years, people were born, lived, and died, being saved only by this promise; the law didn't even exist yet. How then could the law suddenly cancel out the promise? It couldn't. The blessing of Jesus was given as a promise. Salvation in Jesus comes by faith. The law can never change that.

Paul goes on, anticipating the next logical question of his opponents: Then what was the law for? The law was given so that we might recognize our sin. How so? How could we ever name or codify the evil in our hearts without some sort of standard to which we might compare ourselves? How could we clearly understand the holiness of God and our lack of holiness unless there was some code or standard of rightness in the world to hold up as a guideline or measure of goodness? The law showed us our sin until Jesus, the "offspring," came. The law was put in place through Moses, called an "intermediary" here because the two disputing parties (God and humans) needed a mediator.

Of course the law does not contradict the promise; they only have different functions. The law, or "Scripture" in verse 22, "imprisoned everything under sin." As John Calvin wrote, "it shuts up all men under accusation and therefore, instead of giving, it takes away righteousness." The law exists so that we might see that we cannot accomplish it, that we cannot satisfy it. It is only when we realize this truth do we have any motivation to repent and believe in something outside of ourselves for salvation.

Verses 23-26. Paul goes on now to use two metaphors to explain Israel's relationship to the law before Christ came. First, the law was like a jailor, shutting people into the cell of sin, offering them no help to escape. It was guarding Israel, confining her like a prisoner "before faith came." Paul does not mean that no one in the Old Testament Israel had faith; he just finished telling the Gentiles they should emulate the faith of Abraham. He means that they were not able to have faith in the incarnate Christ before he came. Israel was "held captive under the law." For his second metaphor, Paul refers to the law as a guardian in verse 24. He is making reference to the first-century practice of a family hiring someone to be a sort of custodian for a boy from ages seven to seventeen. This person, usually a slave, would have made sure the boy did his chores, acted with right manners and habits, and made it every day to his teacher's house to be taught appropriate lessons for his age. Paul is explaining that the law was this guardian for Israel, working to shape her behavior and ultimately lead her to her true teacher, Christ. The guardian was never expected to be the teacher, only the one who led the boy to the teacher. In the same way, the law was never to give Israel salvation but to lead her to the one who could.

We may be quick to want to change the phrase "sons of God" to "children of God" in verse 26. We shouldn't be. In Paul's world, being a son guaranteed a certain status and a right to the father's inheritance that a daughter would never have. Also, God referred to Israel as his "son" in the Old Testament. The fact that Paul was writing these words to both men and women who were both Jews and Gentiles was revolutionary, and conferred a status on all of them that was unprecedented. Notice there was not a call to "become like" sons of God or to "act like" a son of God. This is a statement of fact: In Christ, we are already God's children, through faith.

Verses 27-29. It may seem here that Paul is equating the ceremonial act of baptism with salvation. In fact, he is using it as a sort of shorthand to refer to everything involved in becoming a believer and living a new life in Christ. New converts often wore white robes to symbolize their new life. Paul may be referring to this as the "putting on" of Christ. The fact that these believers were "in Christ" became their primary identity, before that of Gentile or Jew, slave or free person. Their unity in Christ was more fundamental than their superficial differences. Paul is not telling the Galatians to forget that those in their church have different races or socioeconomic statuses or genders. He is demonstrating the fact that the unity the believers have in Christ takes precedence over anything that might divide them. He is not saying that they should forget their culture, including its practices, music, dress, language, and food. He is saying that culture is secondary to the oneness these believers now enjoy. He is not telling this multi-racial, multi-cultural church to ignore their genders or their different roles or to try to become interchangeable or homogenous. Instead, he is saying that whatever their categories, they are one in Christ. And if they are in Christ, who was Abraham's offspring, they have become heirs of the promise, just as Abraham was. The same is true for our church today. Paul would instruct us not to gloss over our cultural differences but to celebrate them. But he would remind us that any personal identity associations or affiliations must be secondary to the unity we have in Christ.

Chapter 4, verses 1–7. In Paul's day, if a boy's father died when the boy was young, "guardians and managers" handled the affairs of the estate until the boy came of age. While a minor, though the boy technically owned everything, he was not free to exercise any authority. In this way, he was like a slave, subservient, subject to others. The Jews were practicing elementary, ceremonial principles like circumcision and the restriction of certain foods. But then a new era came. "The fullness of time" means God had determined a certain appropriate time for the new era. When that time came, he sent Jesus to be born from the womb of a woman, into a Jewish family. In this way he was fully human and also required to keep the law. He could only buy back those enslaved to the law if he lived under it perfectly. This is the image of redemption: purchasing a slave's freedom. Through his obedience and sacrifice, Jesus bought the freedom of the Jews from the slavery of the law and the freedom of the Gentiles from the slavery of any standard they would try to keep.

Why now does Paul use language of adoption? Redemption and adoption are two parts of our salvation. First he buys our freedom, but he doesn't stop there. He also makes us his children. As Tim Keller explains, "In the Greco-Roman world, a childless, wealthy man could take one of his servants and adopt him. At the moment of adoption, he ceased to be a slave and received all the financial and legal privileges within the estate and outside in the world as the son and heir." This, Paul says, is what God does with us. He buys our freedom through Christ's life and death and then makes us a part of his family, with all of the benefits attached.

But there's still more. He then sends the Holy Spirit into our hearts. While Jesus objectively accomplishes our salvation, legally purchasing for us a status of righteousness, the Holy Spirit personally applies that salvation to us. He helps us feel the love of the Father and know we are his. He stirs our emotions so that the objective truth becomes a subjective experience. We begin to feel the freedom to talk to God like a child would, speaking to him in familial, comfortable terms like "Abba," which roughly translates "Father." As children, we are no longer slaves but legitimate heirs to the promise made hundreds of years ago to Abraham. The Galatians, and we as believers, have gone from rule-following slaves to free, beloved children with an inheritance, all because we are "in Christ."

Reflection Questions

5. How does the analogy of the apple orchard help you understand the relationship of the promise versus the law? In what areas, if any, are you still struggling to understand the relationship between the two?

6. Paul explains through two analogies that the law was both like a jail cell, exposing sin, and a guardian, guiding sinners. In what ways has the law served those roles in your own life?

7. It was revolutionary in Paul's day that both Jews and Gentiles would be given, not earn, the status and benefits of being "sons of God." Does it feel revolutionary in your life today? Why or why not?

8. Paul says that while race, gender, and socioeconomic status matter, our identity should be defined by being "in Christ." Where are you struggling to walk this out in your own, personal areas of identity? Where are you currently resisting this type of unity in the church?

9. Paul makes it clear that we are not just set free from slavery but are adopted and given all the rights of an heir. In what situations do you struggle to believe that you are more than just free but you are also adopted? Why?

Focus verse: *And because you are sons, God has sent the Spirit of his Son into our hearts, crying, "Abba! Father!" So you are no longer a slave, but a son, and if a son, then an heir through God.*
Galatians 4:6–7

Reflections, curiosities, frustrations:

Study 6

Read Galatians 4:8-31

Observation Questions

1. Rewrite verses 8 and 9 in your own words.

2. What do we learn in verses 12–20 about Paul's relationship with the Galatians?

3. In verses 21-31 what differences does Paul point out between Hagar's and Sarah's sons? How does he connect that to the Galatians?

Verses 8-12. In the second half of chapter 4, Paul will return to Abraham and quotes from the Old Testament. But first, he speaks to the Galatians' lack of spiritual growth, and then about his relationship with them. Paul begins by going back to their pre-conversion days. Before they knew the true God, the Galatians probably worshipped "spirit beings," or fake gods that demanded appeasement. But when they came to know God in an intimate way, and, more importantly, to be known by him, they left all of those worthless things. Paul is arguing that by trying to become Jewish in their practice, they were returning to the empty worship they left. Instead of achieving some deeper level of spirituality, they were actually going backward. They were probably observing ceremonial Jewish holy days and other festivals, which would have been quite a commitment and lifestyle change. By doing this, though, they missed the whole point of those ceremonies, which pointed forward to the complete sufficiency of Christ for their salvation. Rather than trusting in Christ, the substance, they were returning to the ceremonial shadows. All of these seemed to be evidence to Paul that these Christians were at risk, that his efforts at preaching Christ to them had been useless. When he tells them to become like him, Paul wants them to become free of the ceremonial law, as he is. In a sense, he became like the Gentiles, not following the Jewish practices he had grown up with.

It is worth noting that there will always be a temptation to trust in our efforts rather than in our God. When we substitute any practice for faith in God, that practice will eventually make us its slave. We long for something that lets us avoid dependence on Christ in our weakness. A program that prescribes three steps to faithfulness or a spiritual discipline to check off our list every day often suits our pride much better than waiting on the Lord by faith.

Verses 13-18. Apparently Paul had some illness or infirmity that was the occasion for his initial visit and stay with the Galatians. At the time, sickness of any kind could have been interpreted as some sort of demon possession. But the Galatians had accepted Paul anyway, welcoming him with honor and respect, as a friend. They had served him sacrificially. Now they seemed to be listening to the agitators among them, the "false brothers," or Judaizers, who may have been telling the Galatians that Paul was their enemy.

Paul had nothing against zeal. But the zeal the Judaizers had for the Galatians was not for their good; it was for the Judaizers' gain. These men wanted the Galatians to isolate themselves from Paul and connect solely to them. They were not motivated by desire to sacrifice for or to love the Galatians, as Paul had been. In fact, this was actually their own attempt to earn their salvation by ministry. Yes, even ministry can be what we look to as the way to earn our right standing with God.

Paul speaks of the Galatians' conversion and growth as a birth, as Christ being formed in them. This is not just an outward change of allegiance in his mind. Being a Christian is a lifelong process of becoming like Christ, "until Christ is formed in you" (verse 19). He had seen the beginnings of this formation when he had been with them before. Now, like a bewildered mother watching her children go astray, he wishes he could speak gently again but must be stern in order to warn them of their clear and present danger.

Verses 21-27. It's as if Paul is saying here, "Are you so sure you even understand this law you want to be under?" The Judaizers would have been very familiar with the story of Sarah and Hagar, and were probably using it in their arguments with the Galatians to convince them they must become Jewish in practice. Paul flips their argument on its head. To understand verses 21-31, we must first remember the story of Sarah and Hagar. Take a minute to read Genesis 16. God had promised Abraham an heir from his own body through a covenant, but many years had passed since then, and still Sarah was not pregnant. So Sarah took things into her own hands by giving her maidservant, Hagar, to Abraham. Basically, Sarah told Abraham to get Hagar pregnant, which he did. This was accomplished solely by natural means, by the will of humans. Because Hagar was a slave (belonging to Abraham as a servant), any of her children would have been considered slaves as well.

Years later, Sarah finally gave birth to Isaac, though she had already gone through menopause. Clearly God intervened to give her a child. Paul is contrasting these two children of Abraham. One, Ishmael, was born to a slave woman, "according to the flesh," with no special intervention by God or miraculous means. Ishmael corresponds to Mount Sinai, where the law was given to Moses and the Israelites. The other child, Isaac, was born "through promise," because God enabled an old woman to become pregnant. Though he does not finish his analogy, we can assume that Paul would have said Isaac corresponds to the covenant God made with Abraham. Paul is telling us that, yes, relation to Abraham is important, but there is a right way to be related to Abraham and a wrong way. You can either resemble his faith from the Spirit or his works done according to the flesh. The resemblance of his faith is the one that identifies you as his heir.

What is all of this talk about Jerusalem? During Paul's day, Jerusalem was the center of Judaism, which relied on the law, not Christ, for salvation. Paul then quotes Isaiah 54, which was originally written to Jewish exiles living in Babylon, who probably believed they would never see Jerusalem as their home, thriving and full of life, again. This Jerusalem was therefore pictured as a barren woman. But God used Isaiah to tell his people that the exile would come to an end and there would be a time of joy for Israel. So, the city would be like a barren woman that became a fertile woman, having many children. This was cause to rejoice. The same was true for Sarah. She, the barren woman, eventually had many descendants.

Verses 28–31. Paul now comes back to Isaac, the child of the promise. Just as Isaac was born as the result of a promise made to Abraham, so his brothers the Galatians were born spiritually as the result of a promise made to Abraham, not because they kept the law. And just as Isaac was persecuted by Ishamel (probably a reference to Genesis 21:9, where Ishmael laughed at Isaac), so children of the promise are always persecuted by children of the slave woman. Tim Keller helps us here: "Paul is flatly stating that the children of the slave—those seeking salvation through law-obedience—will always persecute the children of the free woman—those enjoying salvation by grace. . . . Why is this? Because the gospel is more threatening to religious people than non-religious people."

Sarah eventually told Abraham to throw Hagar out of their camp and into the wilderness with Ishmael. Paul is telling the Galatians that the covenant given at Sinai and the way that it enslaves must be thrown out. Can you hear what he would say to us? "Don't try the way of Hagar! Don't attempt to be born or grow spiritually by meeting a standard, completing a requirement, or living up to an ideal." Whether it is managing your finances a certain way, volunteering at church, achieving a perceived ideal body weight, or any other measurement of stature before God or other people, these are not where you find your identity. None of these are the way to birth or growth as a believer. Only trust in God's promise can make you free. Attempting to please God or find your identity in any other place than his love for you will make you a slave.

Reflection Questions

4. Paul is saddened and shocked by these Christians who had slowed in their spiritual growth due to listening to a false gospel. Have you ever had a season where you have slowed in your spiritual growth for similar reasons? When?

5. Paul had a close, connected relationship to the Galatians at their time of conversion, and now lies and false teachers had caused a painful strain between them. Have you ever experienced that type of heartache with a fellow believer as you have watched them change in similar ways? What is the current status of that relationship?

6. What does it look like practically to depend on Christ in your weakness instead of returning "to the law"?

7. Tim Keller says that "the gospel is more threatening to religious people than non-religious people." What do you think this means, and have you found this to be true?

8. What is the current thing that you are using in the Jesus + something equation to get favor from God instead of resting by faith in his love? What do you need to repent of?

Focus verse: *But now that you have come to know God, or rather to be known by God, how can you turn back again to the weak and worthless elementary principles of the world, whose slaves you want to be once more?*
Galatians 4:9

Reflections, curiosities, frustrations:

Study 7

Read Galatians 5

Observation Questions

1. In verses 1-6 what is Paul again telling them about circumcision and following the law?

2. In verses 7-12 what is Paul confident will happen to the Galatians? What does he want to happen to those who misled them?

3. Write the list of the works of the flesh versus works of the Spirit (verses 16-26).

Verses 1-6. All of Galatians could be summed up in verse 1. "Stand firm" is the translation of a Greek word from the military world, commanding the church in Galatia to be alert and strong together while resisting attacks on their faith. These were indeed attacks, as the Judaizers attempted to turn these brothers and sisters away from the gospel to some other system of relating to God. At one time they were pagans, slaves to false gods. Paul is telling them that if they "accept circumcision," making it a badge of honor, they will once again be in bondage, this time to the law. It seems that these believers had already begun practicing some aspects of Judaism, like celebrating seasons and holy days, but they had not yet been circumcised. Paul is saying these brothers, instead of taking a step toward intimacy with God, would actually be turning away from God and back to a religion of slavery if they were circumcised. He is essentially saying that there are two paths toward righteousness: the path of working for God's acceptance and the path of grace. If you get circumcised, you have chosen the path of works-righteousness, and you have no place for God's grace.

What the leaders of the Judaizers may not have been telling the Galatians was that not only would they have to celebrate holy days and be circumcised but they would also have to keep, perfectly, all 613 laws the Jews held up from the Old Testament.

Since that requirement is impossible for us to keep, this system could never be the way to salvation.

Paul's words here about circumcision would have sounded radical to his audience. As opposed to those saying that there is a complicated moral code that we must follow to the letter in order to be saved, Paul is telling these brothers and us that it is love enabled by the Spirit that must dictate our actions. Our faith works itself out through Spirit-empowered love, not law-keeping. Elsewhere, Paul was willing to circumcise Timothy in order to gain access to share the gospel of Jesus with unbelieving Jews, who would not associate with anyone uncircumcised (Acts 16:3). Here, though, these were professing Christians insisting upon circumcision. If Paul went along with it, circumcision would enslave Gentile believers to the ceremonial law and distort the gospel.

Verses 7-12. Paul uses one of his favorite images for the Christian life: a running race. The Galatians were making good progress, growing by faith. But someone stepped in and hindered them, becoming an obstacle in their running path. "A little leaven leavens the whole lump" was a well-known proverb in Paul's day. Leaven, which had yeastlike properties, was often used to cause an entire lump of dough to rise. It would work its way through the flour until the whole of it was affected. In the same way, Paul was seeing the influence of a few false brothers working its way through the Galatian church. And yet he had confidence that the recipients of his letter would see the lies of the Judaizers for what they were, and that the agitators would be penalized by God for what they were doing. Notice that Paul was confident that there would be punishment and penalty for any who attempted to add requirements for salvation other than trusting in Christ to the gospel. We must be very careful that we do not put a heavy burden on any brother or sister by insisting on some sort of performance as a way to earn God's pleasure.

Apparently, because Paul had allowed Timothy to be circumcised (see Acts 16), some were saying that he was preaching circumcision. Paul argues that if he were, the Jews and the Judaizers would not be so angry with him. He was preaching not circumcision but the cross, which is always offensive. The cross boldly proclaims to every human that they cannot save themselves. It tells us that we need a savior, which is extremely insulting to a proud heart. Paul finishes his words about circumcision with a crude and bold statement. In effect, he is saying that if these agitators were going to make such a big deal about cutting off a small piece of flesh, he wishes they would just go ahead and cut off the entire organ. He may have been making a reference to some priests of Cybele, a goddess. Some of them apparently cut off their testicles in service to their deity.

Verses 13–15. Here comes a big shift. Most of Paul's letter has been about the Galatians' relationship with the law and the fact that they were saved by faith and grew by faith, not by being more Jewish or more law-abiding. We could use one word to summarize this way of thinking, that following the rules can save you: *legalism.* If Christianity is running down a road to glory, we must avoid falling into the ditch of legalism on one side. But there is another ditch on the other side of the road: *license.* The freedom that Paul has been explaining throughout this letter is freedom from the bondage of trying to reach a standard. But this freedom is a very different thing than the idea of self-rule, which our culture glorifies. Christ did not free us so that we might go and serve ourselves, obeying no one. In fact, the word he uses for "serve" in verse 13 in the phrase "but through love serve one another" is actually the word "slave." When Christ frees us from our slavery to the Jewish ceremonial law or any other standard to attain a good standing before him, he does so in order that we might become slaves to one another. We have been freed from our own bondage to sin so that we actually have the opportunity to love someone else. This is impossible without God's intervention in the heart of a human. Paul's words about biting and devouring present a picture of wild animals, serving only themselves. He is probably referring to specific interactions happening in the Galatian church. Instead of this fighting, which is self-centered, Paul is calling these brothers to a life constrained by love, which is self-sacrificing.

Verses 16–21. Self-sacrifice does not come easily. We do not naturally want to love other people, put them first, or give up anything so that they might flourish. Without some sort of intervention, it is impossible for us to do anything but indulge our own desires. Though the Galatians had been freed from the bondage of serving the law or any other standard to win God's approval, were they and are we now to be stuck in the bondage of pleasing ourselves? Thank God, there is another way—the way of the Spirit. We have not been left alone to fight our lust for and idolatry of the good things God made. Instead, we have been given the Holy Spirit, who lives in us, enabling us to walk out the life of faith.

Though the word "desires" in verse 17 is actually neutral, our sinful nature corrupts our desires, twisting them away from God. These are longings that drive and control us. Often they are not for evil things but for good gifts that God has given: beauty, sex, comfort, intimacy, and so on. But our flesh turns these good things into ultimate things or idols that we demand from God. The reality is that there are two natures (and, therefore, two sets of desires) at work in us: the flesh and the Holy Spirit. They are at war within us every moment of every day. However, there is a strong hope given to us in verse 17: "to keep you from doing the things you want to do." Paul is telling us that the most true thing about us, the thing that characterizes us as believers, is the desire to please God. It may be frayed, failing, and weak at times, but it is the real ambition of our hearts—to love God. This is the work of the Spirit, who rejects the idolatry we make of the good things of this world and instead turns our desires toward Jesus.

Paul uses the word *flesh*, or *sarx*, very deliberately in his letters. Here he describes the things people do when controlled by the twisted desires of their flesh. Lists of unacceptable behavior, like the one Paul uses here, were common in this era. Sex between unmarried people was common in first-century Roman culture, as was a widespread sexual "openness" that surrounded the Galatian church. Sensuality refers to wild living, the life of one who lives only for the next party. Idolatry was worshipping anything other than God. Sorcery was related first to the giving of poison and other drugs while practicing magic but then to the use of magic itself. Enmity is hatred and the expressions of it, which lead to strife —bickering and fighting. Fits of rage are outbursts of anger.

The drunkenness in verse 21 refers to going on a bender, a drinking binge. The orgies listed here are not only sexual, though they can lead to that. This word was originally used to refer to the feasts given in honor of Greek gods that usually involved a lot of alcohol and then sexual pleasuring. Notice that Paul was not writing to a group of extremely self-disciplined, pristine people who knew nothing of sin or the things that happen under the influence of alcohol at night. The gospel of grace is available to people with any sort of history. Notice also that God, through Paul, does not elevate the importance of the "dirtier" or "worse" external sins involving drugs, sex, and screaming fights, like we often do. He puts them right next to the more "acceptable," church-people sins of envy, jealousy, dissensions, and rivalries. (Consider your last "discussion" in a church setting about worship music preferences or political leanings.) All of these are the result of being controlled by our flesh. This is what characterizes a life led by our own unchecked human desires. Paul is not talking about the occasional struggles and lapses of a believer. Of course we fail. We repent, believe again how we are loved by our God, accept his forgiveness, and continue walking by the Spirit. Paul is giving a list of habitual sins that characterize one who lives only by their flesh. The fruit of being led only by our sinful desires is rotten indeed.

Verses 22-26. Life lived by the power of the Holy Spirit looks different. Instead of demanding things, the Spirit produces things. What things? What Paul gives us here is probably not an exhaustive list describing a Spirit-led life; he probably chose these in particular to speak to the situation of the Galatians. These are also not expected to be divided up among believers, giving one love, another peace, and another joy. "Fruit" is singular, meaning that if we are led by and living in the Spirit, what will be produced in each of us is a whole crop of things.

Love is first and most important, and probably the biggest antidote to the agitation happening in the Galatian church. Leon Morris gives us an excellent definition of joy: "a settled state of mind that arises from a sense of God's love for us, produced by the spirit and that exists even in the face of difficulties and trials." Peace probably refers here to peace between believers. Patience is like the patience God shows to us. Gentleness or meekness comes from "not being overly impressed by a sense of one's importance," which was perfectly displayed by Jesus. Faith probably refers to faithfulness to God. Kindness involves not asserting ourselves when it is unnecessary. Self-control stands in opposition to the self-gratification listed in the works of the flesh. Not only is there no law against any of these things; these are the qualities and characteristics whereby we actually fulfill the law.

If you are in Christ (which you are if you're a believer), Paul declares that you have crucified the flesh. Romans 6:6 helps us here: "We know that our old self was crucified with him in order that the body of sin might be brought to nothing, so that we would no longer be enslaved to sin." Remember, because we are in Christ, everything that is his is now ours. All of his accomplishments are now our accomplishments. We have crucified the flesh and its constant demands to be pleasured and served. The power our flesh had over us has been broken. While it continues to tempt us, it is no longer what controls us. We now have the ability, by the Spirit, to repent from, resist, and put to death its quiet lure. This is an ongoing crucifixion. We do not sit back and passively assume that all is finished. Yes, the Spirit begins and completes the work, but we are constantly responding to him as he prompts, convicts, and leads. We must stop when he warns, turn away from sin when he convicts, and move forward in love when he prompts. On the other hand, we do not need to be anxiously hypervigilant, assuming that the responsibility of holiness depends solely on us. We can be assured that God will complete the work that he has begun in us by his Spirit. Paul is leading the Galatians and us to always be asking if we are responding to the Spirit as he leads. Are these the things that maybe not perfectly but consistently characterize our lives? It is not so much one of these vices or virtues but the combination of them in a continual way that declares either Christ or ourselves as seated on the throne of our hearts.

Reflection Questions

4. Why does choosing a path of works–righteousness leave no room for grace?

5. Paul tells them that it should be not a moral code that drives us but love enabled through the Spirit. What does this look like practically? Can you give an example?

6. We have been freed from bondage to sin not to just serve self but to love and care for others. Do you use this freedom in this way? Why or why not?

7. The desires of the flesh are corrupted by sin and twisted away from God. Sometimes, the flesh does not desire bad things but transforms our desires for good things into idols. Where are you currently struggling with idolatrous desires that are taking up too much space in your life? What do you need to repent of? To whom do you need to confess?

8. As you interact with the Spirit, how can you tell when you are living by the Spirit or living by the flesh? What does it look like to lean into the Spirit and ask for help in all things?

Focus verse: *For through the Spirit, by faith, we ourselves eagerly wait for the hope of righteousness. For in Christ Jesus neither circumcision nor uncircumcision counts for anything, but only faith working through love.*
Galatians 5:5–6

Reflections, curiosities, frustrations:

Study 8

Boast in the Cross

Read Galatians 6

Observation Questions

1. In verses 1-5 what things does Paul call believers to do for each other? What attitude toward themselves does he call them to have?

2. In verses 6-10 what does Paul say about the Spirit and the flesh? What things does he exhort them to do?

3. In verses 11-18 what point does Paul drive home one more time? What words does he use to do this?

Verses 1-5. Before we walk through this chapter, remember the atmosphere and context into which Paul was sending this letter. This group of people had been saved by grace through faith, but they were being told by a number of false brothers that in order to really be Christians they had to add something to Jesus's work. Imagine the climate this would have produced. People would have judged one another by outward accomplishments, sizing up their actions at every turn. This teaching would have encouraged arrogance on the part of those who were disciplined in keeping the Jewish, ceremonial law. It would have fostered a climate of distrust and comparison.

Paul's words shift the goal of these brothers from out-accomplishing one another to supporting one another. Instead of looking at a brother or sister who fell into sin as someone they could "beat" in their spiritual "race," the Galatians were to stop and help them up, enabling them to get back into the race. "You who are spiritual" simply refers to those who are indwelt by the Holy Spirit—all Christians. It is the job of every believer, when they see a certain sin has gotten control of a sister, to gently lead her toward repentance so that she can be restored. The word translated "restore" could have been used in the sense of setting a broken bone, restoring it to its right place in the body. In this sense, we are our sister's keeper. But while we do this, we must be careful that we are not tempted—not necessarily in the same way that our sister was, but tempted to feel superior to her in this situation, that somehow we are above her because we did not get caught in this same sin at this time.

The burdens we are told to bear may stem from the situation the brother or sister was facing in verse 1, being caught in a sin. But that is not where our responsibility ends. We are to help those with whom we worship in all matters, from house hunting to marriage problems, carpools to heart attacks, party planning to sitting in grief together. As we do these things, we fulfill the law of Christ. These are the ethical demands of the gospel, the necessity of service to others to which Jesus calls all believers. His life of service and love fulfilled the law. As Tim Keller writes, "We bear others' burdens because Christ bore ours."

In verse 3 Paul is not telling us that we are worthless. He is saying that in terms of saving ourselves, we have nothing to offer; we are totally dependent on Jesus. And even beyond that, anything we do to serve God is only the result of our dependence on the Spirit. We "test" our own work not by comparing it to what other people around us do or accomplish or how they obey but by considering our own faithfulness in what God has given to us as our responsibility. The word translated "load" was used for the cargo of a ship, which each ship had to deliver to its destination. While these believers were to assist one another in the life of faith, Paul was reminding them that they would ultimately stand before God and answer on the Day of Judgment only for how they handled their own load. We will do the same. Because of this, comparison of our behavior or of our circumstances to that of other believers is simply a waste of time.

Verses 6–8. The "one who is taught the word" refers to all of the new converts who were being instructed in basic Christian doctrine. Remember that in Paul's day no church systems existed.

There were no official pastor positions that came with a salary or benefits. Those who catechized, or taught, the new believers were providing the foundation for the faith of the brothers and sisters. But these people also needed to eat. We have no record of whether the teachers were given food, money, or a place to stay. But Paul is telling the students, who would have been mostly adults, that it is their duty to be sure their teachers are cared for. In verse 7, Paul warns the believers that they must take the Word of God that they're learning seriously. A judgment is coming, and God cannot be ignored without serious consequences. Just as a farmer who sows barley reaps barley, so a person who invests in the flesh and all of its lusts will reap the harvest of corruption, meaning eternal death. A person who invests in the Spirit will eventually be resurrected. Paul is not saying here that we earn our salvation. He is saying that just as there are physical consequences and structure to the universe, so there are moral consequences and structure. Just as gravity pulls the apple to the ground, so lying has a consequence of degrading trust between two people. Those who are in Christ have been redeemed, but the pull of sin is still very real until final redemption takes place and all is made right. Paul encourages us in this fight between our flesh and the Holy Spirit to respond to the Spirit and reap the good consequences.

Verses 9–10. The work of a believer is long and tiring. Faithfulness to God brings trouble in this world. Our walk of faith is a marathon, not a sprint, and it can be full of discouragement and trials. Paul encourages the Galatians and us that eventually, whether in this lifetime or in the new heavens and earth, we will see the fruit of our labors in the kingdom. We will see people come to faith and grow to be more like Christ. We will see the results of the money we've given, the time we've sacrificed to serve the church, the physical help we've provided, and the hours we've spent in prayer. We must not give up. In fact, we must do good here on earth while we can, while we have the opportunity. Most immediately, we must help our brothers and sisters in the family of God.

There was no welfare state in Paul's day. The poor Christians in the church could beg, but there was not much help beyond that. Because of this reality, the early Christians took helping the poor very seriously. Though our physical and financial reality may be slightly different because of government or other programs, the same command holds from Paul. In the scope of our existence, we will spend a very small fraction of it on earth. We have only these few years to do good to those around us, in the midst of pain and brokenness. In the new heavens and earth, there will be no need for this help, for doctors, counselors, social workers, EMTs, or any other help for neighbors or sisters in pain. All will have been healed. The time that we have to serve Jesus by doing good to other Christians is now.

Verses 11-13. Paul usually dictated letters to a scribe but then often wrote the final portion with his own hand in order to prove its authenticity. With his final words he gets to the heart of the issue: the false teachers cared more about what others thought than they did about the true gospel. At the time in Rome, Judaism was recognized and accepted by the Roman state, and the preachers who advocated for circumcision aligned themselves just closely enough to the Jews to avoid persecution. Instead of preaching Christ to save sinners and give him glory, the Judaizers were attempting to get glory for themselves by convincing men to be circumcised.

Verses 14-16. No polite Roman citizen would have mentioned the word *crucifixion* in conversation but would have used a euphemism instead. But Paul did not avoid speaking of the crucifixion. In fact, he boasted in it. It was the thing that told him who he was, that provided his identity, that gave him worth. Because Jesus had been crucified, the world was dead to Paul; it no longer had any power over him. It was not only that circumcision didn't count for anything in the pursuit of favor with God; uncircumcision didn't count for anything either. It was not required to join the people of God, to please God, or to be saved by God.

"New creation" was a technical term that referred to the new world that Jews believed would come after the world was either destroyed or renewed. Paul is saying that this "new creation" was happening now, in those who were in Christ, who were therefore indwelt by the Holy Spirit. This is the church, the "Israel of God" that he mentions in verse 16. The old Israel was one nation given the Old Covenant. The Israel of God here includes both Jews and Gentiles, and eventually every tribe and tongue.

Paul makes one final reference to the analogy of the Christian life as a walk, and then refers to a "rule." Hasn't he just written an entire letter pointing the Galatians away from rules? This word also can refer to a straight rod, a standard, like our yardstick. These Christians were no longer to try to become Jewish or observe Jewish laws, but this did not mean that there was no standard by which to live. The ceremonial laws of circumcision, sacrifices, and Jewish festivals pointed forward to Christ, and were fulfilled by Christ, so that we no longer need to keep those laws. Christ also fulfilled the moral law, as summarized in the Ten Commandments, but that fulfillment was different. Christ fulfilled the external obligations of the moral law so that he might write that law directly onto our hearts, by the work of the Holy Spirit. Christ gives us the moral law not to earn salvation but as a guide for the one who has it.

Verses 17-18. Paul takes one last opportunity to mention grace, the source of salvation. While the Judaizers were attempting to gain a reputation for themselves, Paul's only reputation was for talking about Jesus and his cross. While the false brothers wanted the trophies of circumcised men's bodies, Paul had scars on his body from being beaten for preaching the cross. While the Judaizers added to the gospel to avoid persecution, Paul boldly preached Christ crucified for salvation. Did he preach and live this way because he was so amazing? Because he was a super apostle? Because he had achieved a level of favor with God above the others? No. He did so because he had aligned himself with Jesus and found a Savior. Because he had seen Jesus's beauty and majesty and would not allow anything else but him to be worshipped. Because he longed for his brothers and sisters in Galatia to know freedom from the law and any other crippling standard like he had come to know.

Even now Paul would say to us, "Do you want to be a real Christian? Believe the gospel. Do you desire to grow in your faith? Respond to God's grace by studying the Word and praying not because you want to earn God's favor but because you already have it." Don't be fooled by those offering an improvement plan that is motivated by anything other than the fact that Jesus's death and resurrection has already made you right with God. Don't look around at your sisters and compare your life, spiritual discipline, or church attendance to theirs. When your sin seems overwhelming, look at the cross and know you don't need to add anything to the work Jesus has already done. Certainly, crucify the desires of the flesh, and cultivate the desires of the Spirit, but do so in the power of the Holy Spirit, not your own. When your sister makes a decision you disagree with about schooling for her children or what politician she will support, believe the gospel and let her stand firm in her freedom. Stand firm in the freedom Christ won for you and do not submit to the opinions of others, to a cultural standard, or to any other yoke of slavery. You were saved and you will grow by faith in Jesus alone. Glory in his crucifixion and stand firm in your freedom.

Reflection Questions

4. Paul encourages the Galatians to care for one another in their struggles against sin. When have you struggled to care for your sister in Christ because you looked down on a particular sin struggle she had? How do Paul's words guide your heart for the future?

5. Two groups that Paul mentions helping are those teaching the Scriptures and the poor. Why was that important at that time in history? What does that look like in your life currently?

6. While the Judiazers' behavior was rooted in building a reputation for themselves, Paul was ministering to the Galatians to spread Jesus's reputation. When you think about your current role at your church, whose reputation are you most concerned with? Why?

7. Paul uses the phrase "new creation" to describe what is happening now for those who are in Christ. Define the words *new* and *creation*. Where do you see these definitions show up in your life because of the work of the Spirit?

8. Re-read the last paragraph in the commentary again. In the various things listed that we might be struggling with, which one most resonated with your heart? Why? Write a prayer for that area of your life.

9. What are your main takeaways from your time studying the book of Galatians?

Focus verse: *But far be it from me to boast except in the cross of our Lord Jesus Christ, by which the world has been crucified to me, and I to the world. For neither circumcision counts for anything, nor uncircumcision, but a new creation.*
Galatians 6:14–15

Reflections, curiosities, frustrations:

Acknowledgments

Christine: Michael, once again you have been the one to check in on me all throughout this book and be my sounding board. Your patience with me has not gone unnoticed, and I am thankful for you. Robbie (Dr. Robert Griggs), you have been generous with your time and enjoyable to learn from, especially on my back porch. The respect you have shown me in this process has been life-giving. Renae, I cannot tell you how much it matters that you keep showing up. Jen, I hope you know that your encouragement and prayers are not a side benefit in this thing; they're running this thing. Jacob, thank you once again for your faithfulness to us.

Hope: Ray-ray, you always cheer me on and remind me of what it is all for. Chris, your ability to do mental gymnastics with this hard text amazes me, and I love walking this road with you. To Renae and Jen— you guys make the best team. Love that we can be real and laugh hard in the same sitting. Tulsa forever. Jesus, I am beyond thankful that I don't have to add anything to your work on the cross.

Notes

1. Deserting the Gospel of Grace: Galatians 1:1-10

9   "The book of Galatians is dynamite": Keller, *Galatians for You*, 9.

3. Did Christ Die for Nothing? Galatians 2:11-21

32   "If anyone could be saved by being good": Keller, *Galatians for You*, 61.

5. From Slave to Son: Galatians 3:15-4:7

50   "it shuts up all men under accusation": Calvin qtd. in Morris, *Galatians*, 116.
53   "In the Greco-Roman world": Keller, *Galatians for You*, 98.

6. Why Are You Turning Back? Galatians 4:8-31

63   "Paul is flatly stating": Keller, *Galatians for You*, 128.

7. Freedom and the Spirit: Galatians 5

75   Instead of demanding things: Moo, *Galatians*, 363.
75   "a settled state of mind": Ibid., 364.
75   "not being overly impressed": Ibid., 366.

8. Boast in the Cross: Galatians 6

83   "We bear others' burdens": Keller, *Galatians for You*, 169.
86   "New creation" was a technical term: Moo, *Galatians*, 398.

Works Cited

Keller, Timothy. *Galatians for You*. Epsom, Surrey, England: The Good Book Company, 2013.

Moo, Douglas J. *Galatians*. Baker Exegetical Commentary on the New Testament. Grand Rapids, MI: Baker Academic, 2013.

Morris, Leon. *Galatians: Paul's Charter of Christian Freedom*. Downers Grove, IL: Intervarsity Press, 1996.

Other At His Feet Studies

We pray that you will continue to sit at the feet of Jesus, studying his Word. To help you with this, we have also written Bible studies for women on these books of the Bible:

Romans (28 studies)

1 Samuel (16 studies)

Philippians (12 studies)

Psalms (13 studies)

Luke: Part 1 (13 studies)

Luke: Part 2 (14 studies)

Luke: Part 3 (12 studies)

Made in the USA
Coppell, TX
27 January 2022

72490458R00062